Henry Hudson

Jane Gould

PowerKiDS

Published in 2013 by The Rosen Publishing Group, Inc.

29 East 21st Street, New York, NY 10010

First Edition

Editor: Joanne Randolph

Book Design: Planman Technologies

Illustrations: Planman Technologies

Library of Congress Cataloging-in-Publication Data

Gould, Jane H.

Henry Hudson / by Jane Gould. — 1st ed.

    p. cm. — (Jr. graphic famous explorers)

Includes index.

ISBN 978-1-4777-0071-6 (library binding) — ISBN 978-1-4777-0127-0 (pbk.) — ISBN 978-1-4777-0128-7 (6-pack)

1. Hudson, Henry, d. 1611—Juvenile literature. 2. America—Discovery and exploration—British—Juvenile literature.
3. Explorers—America—Biography—Juvenile literature.
4. Explorers—Great Britain—Biography—Juvenile literature. I. Title.

E129.H8G68 2013

910.92—dc23

[B]

2012018693

Manufactured in the United States of America

CPSIA Compliance Information: Batch #WR31422IRC: For further information contact Rosen Publishing, New York, New York at 1-800-237-9932.

Contents

Introduction

Henry Hudson lived during the Elizabethan era. Many think of it as a golden age of English history. Queen Elizabeth ruled the land, and William Shakespeare wrote his famous plays during this time. Many brave men also risked their lives to explore the new, unmapped lands called the Americas. The discoveries of these explorers changed the way Europeans saw the world. Hudson dreamed of finding a new northern route to Asia. Despite many dangers, he stopped at nothing to find the **Northwest Passage**.

Main Characters

John Davis (c. 1550–1605) A British explorer and **navigator** who searched for the Northwest Passage to Asia. Hudson might have served on one of his voyages.

Henry Greene (c. 1580–c. 1611) A crew member on the *Discovery*. He was one of the leaders of the **mutiny** against Hudson.

Henry Hudson (c. 1565–1611) A British explorer who continued the search for a northern route across the Atlantic Ocean from Europe to Asia. He led four voyages in his attempts to find a route.

Robert Juet (c. 1500s–1600s) A crew member on three of Hudson's voyages. He was one of the leaders of the mutiny against Hudson.

Samuel Purchase (c. 1500s–1600s) A geographer and friend of Henry Hudson.

HENRY HUDSON

HENRY HUDSON WAS AN ENGLISH EXPLORER WHO WAS **OBSESSED** WITH FINDING A NORTHERN **TRADE** ROUTE TO ASIA. HE SPENT MUCH OF HIS LIFE SEARCHING FOR IT.

HUDSON WAS BORN NEAR LONDON AROUND 1565. NO ONE IS SURE OF THE EXACT YEAR. LITTLE IS KNOWN ABOUT HIS FAMILY OR EARLY LIFE. MANY PEOPLE BELIEVE THAT HUDSON'S FAMILY WORKED AS TRADERS.

HENRY, FIND THE SILK CLOTH FROM INDIA. WE SHOULD HAVE THREE CRATES OF IT.

HERE IS ONE, FATHER.

YOUR COUSIN IS THE CAPTAIN, AND HE IS SAILING TO RUSSIA. HE SAID YOU COULD BE HIS CABIN BOY.

I WOULD LIKE THAT, FATHER. MAYBE I CAN LEARN NAVIGATION!

MOST LIKELY, HIS FAMILY USED **MERCHANT** SHIPS TO CARRY GOODS. HENRY WAS PROBABLY A BOY WHEN HE FIRST WENT TO SEA.

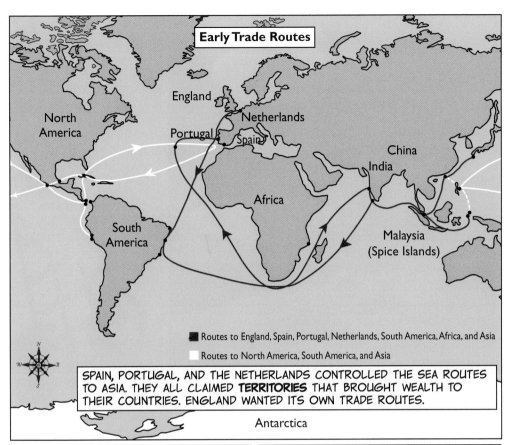

Early Trade Routes

England
Netherlands
Portugal
Spain
North America
South America
Africa
China
India
Malaysia (Spice Islands)
Antarctica

◼ Routes to England, Spain, Portugal, Netherlands, South America, Africa, and Asia
◻ Routes to North America, South America, and Asia

SPAIN, PORTUGAL, AND THE NETHERLANDS CONTROLLED THE SEA ROUTES TO ASIA. THEY ALL CLAIMED **TERRITORIES** THAT BROUGHT WEALTH TO THEIR COUNTRIES. ENGLAND WANTED ITS OWN TRADE ROUTES.

MERCHANTS BROUGHT **PRECIOUS** METALS, SPICES, AND CLOTH FROM INDIA, CHINA, MALAYSIA, AND OTHER PARTS OF ASIA.

PEPPER SELLS VERY WELL. I WILL BUY AS MUCH AS YOU CAN GIVE ME. DO YOU HAVE ANY **CLOVES**?

RICH **INVESTORS** PAID EXPLORERS TO FIND NEW SEA ROUTES TO ASIA. MANY HOPED TO FIND A NORTHERN WATER PASSAGE.

DO YOU THINK WE WOULD LOSE FEWER SHIPS WITH A NORTHERN ROUTE?

IT WOULD BE LESS DANGEROUS THAN A TRIP AROUND AFRICA OR SOUTH AMERICA, AND IT WOULD BE SHORTER.

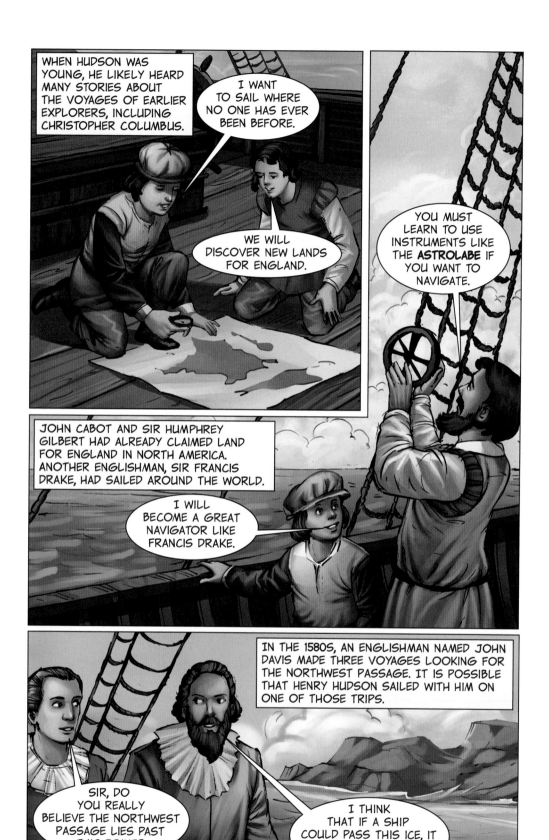

WHEN HUDSON WAS YOUNG, HE LIKELY HEARD MANY STORIES ABOUT THE VOYAGES OF EARLIER EXPLORERS, INCLUDING CHRISTOPHER COLUMBUS.

I WANT TO SAIL WHERE NO ONE HAS EVER BEEN BEFORE.

WE WILL DISCOVER NEW LANDS FOR ENGLAND.

YOU MUST LEARN TO USE INSTRUMENTS LIKE THE **ASTROLABE** IF YOU WANT TO NAVIGATE.

JOHN CABOT AND SIR HUMPHREY GILBERT HAD ALREADY CLAIMED LAND FOR ENGLAND IN NORTH AMERICA. ANOTHER ENGLISHMAN, SIR FRANCIS DRAKE, HAD SAILED AROUND THE WORLD.

I WILL BECOME A GREAT NAVIGATOR LIKE FRANCIS DRAKE.

IN THE 1580S, AN ENGLISHMAN NAMED JOHN DAVIS MADE THREE VOYAGES LOOKING FOR THE NORTHWEST PASSAGE. IT IS POSSIBLE THAT HENRY HUDSON SAILED WITH HIM ON ONE OF THOSE TRIPS.

SIR, DO YOU REALLY BELIEVE THE NORTHWEST PASSAGE LIES PAST THIS POINT?

I THINK THAT IF A SHIP COULD PASS THIS ICE, IT COULD SAIL ALL THE WAY TO ASIA.

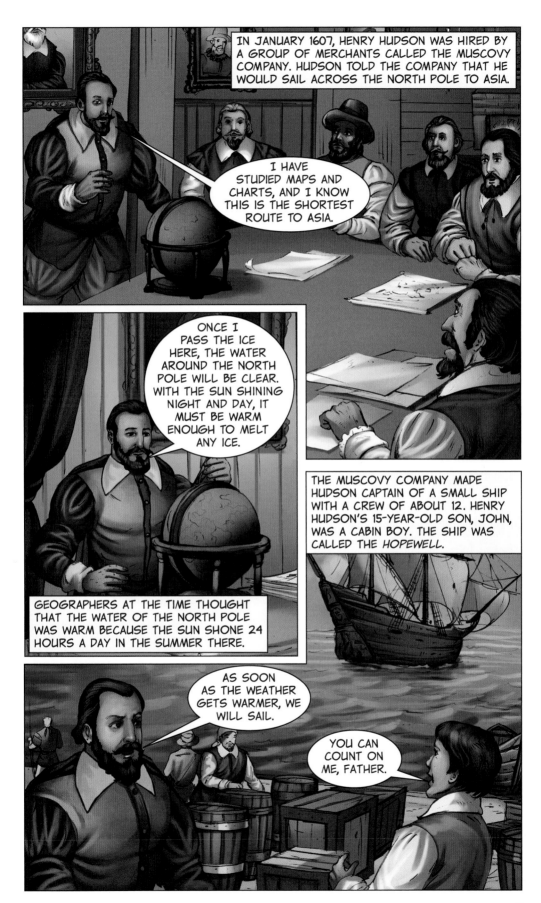

IN JANUARY 1607, HENRY HUDSON WAS HIRED BY A GROUP OF MERCHANTS CALLED THE MUSCOVY COMPANY. HUDSON TOLD THE COMPANY THAT HE WOULD SAIL ACROSS THE NORTH POLE TO ASIA.

I HAVE STUDIED MAPS AND CHARTS, AND I KNOW THIS IS THE SHORTEST ROUTE TO ASIA.

ONCE I PASS THE ICE HERE, THE WATER AROUND THE NORTH POLE WILL BE CLEAR. WITH THE SUN SHINING NIGHT AND DAY, IT MUST BE WARM ENOUGH TO MELT ANY ICE.

THE MUSCOVY COMPANY MADE HUDSON CAPTAIN OF A SMALL SHIP WITH A CREW OF ABOUT 12. HENRY HUDSON'S 15-YEAR-OLD SON, JOHN, WAS A CABIN BOY. THE SHIP WAS CALLED THE *HOPEWELL*.

GEOGRAPHERS AT THE TIME THOUGHT THAT THE WATER OF THE NORTH POLE WAS WARM BECAUSE THE SUN SHONE 24 HOURS A DAY IN THE SUMMER THERE.

AS SOON AS THE WEATHER GETS WARMER, WE WILL SAIL.

YOU CAN COUNT ON ME, FATHER.

7

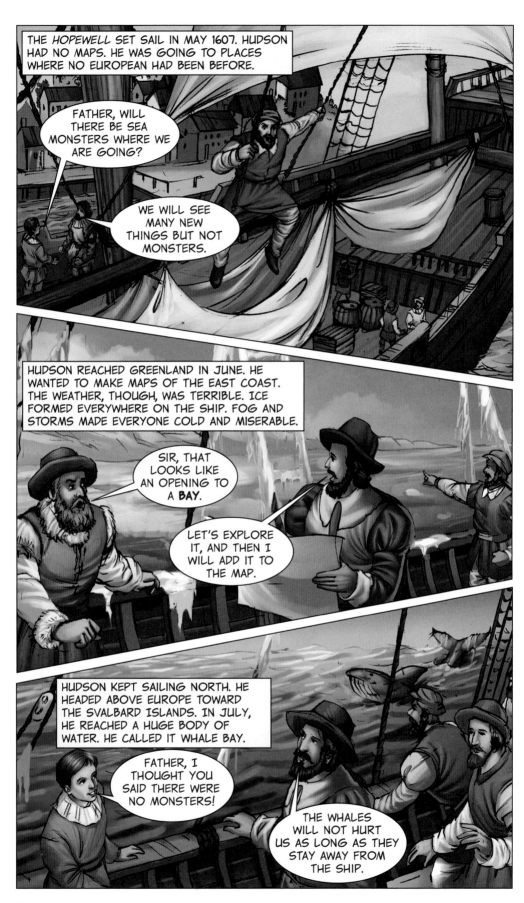

THE *HOPEWELL* SET SAIL IN MAY 1607. HUDSON HAD NO MAPS. HE WAS GOING TO PLACES WHERE NO EUROPEAN HAD BEEN BEFORE.

FATHER, WILL THERE BE SEA MONSTERS WHERE WE ARE GOING?

WE WILL SEE MANY NEW THINGS BUT NOT MONSTERS.

HUDSON REACHED GREENLAND IN JUNE. HE WANTED TO MAKE MAPS OF THE EAST COAST. THE WEATHER, THOUGH, WAS TERRIBLE. ICE FORMED EVERYWHERE ON THE SHIP. FOG AND STORMS MADE EVERYONE COLD AND MISERABLE.

SIR, THAT LOOKS LIKE AN OPENING TO A **BAY**.

LET'S EXPLORE IT, AND THEN I WILL ADD IT TO THE MAP.

HUDSON KEPT SAILING NORTH. HE HEADED ABOVE EUROPE TOWARD THE SVALBARD ISLANDS. IN JULY, HE REACHED A HUGE BODY OF WATER. HE CALLED IT WHALE BAY.

FATHER, I THOUGHT YOU SAID THERE WERE NO MONSTERS!

THE WHALES WILL NOT HURT US AS LONG AS THEY STAY AWAY FROM THE SHIP.

HUDSON WAS FEWER THAN 600 MILES (1,000 KM) FROM THE NORTH POLE. HE STILL HOPED TO FIND A WARM NORTHERN OCEAN.

THIS SHIP CANNOT PASS THROUGH THIS ICE.

WE MUST TRY. I'M SURE THERE WILL BE OPEN SEAS NORTH OF HERE.

PUSH HARDER, MEN! WE ARE ALMOST FREE OF IT!

IF WE SURVIVE THIS, I WILL NOT GO ANY FARTHER.

NONE OF US WILL.

HUDSON RETURNED TO ENGLAND IN SEPTEMBER 1607. HE THOUGHT HIS TRIP HAD BEEN A FAILURE. THE MUSCOVY COMPANY SAW A WAY TO GET RICH, THOUGH. THE DISCOVERY OF WHALE BAY LED TO THE BEGINNING OF ENGLAND'S WHALING INDUSTRY.

HUGE ICE **FLOES** CLOSED IN AROUND THE SHIP. THE SHIP WAS IN DANGER OF BEING CRUSHED. FORTUNATELY, A STRONG WIND PUSHED THE SHIP INTO OPEN WATER.

WE WILL PAY YOU WHATEVER YOU WANT TO LEAD A WHALING EXPEDITION.

NO. I WILL NOT GIVE UP ON FINDING A NEW NORTHERN ROUTE.

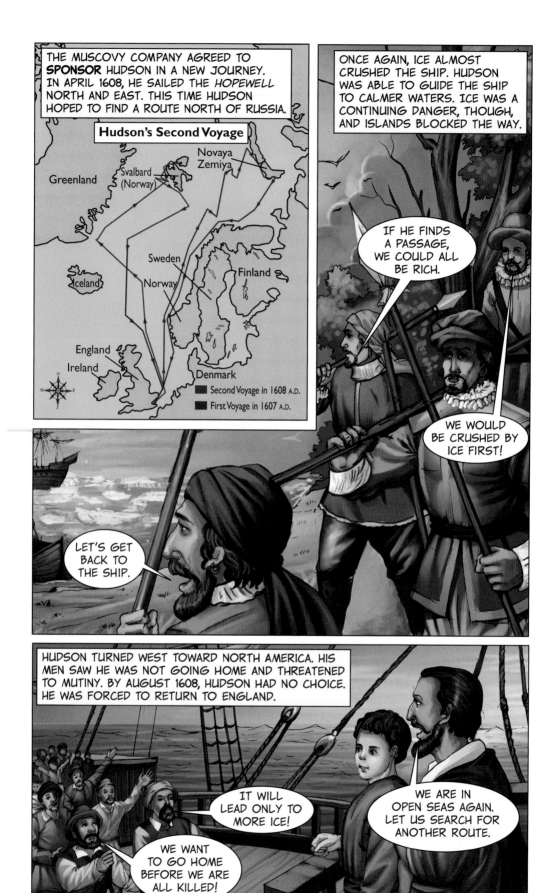

THE MUSCOVY COMPANY AGREED TO **SPONSOR** HUDSON IN A NEW JOURNEY. IN APRIL 1608, HE SAILED THE *HOPEWELL* NORTH AND EAST. THIS TIME HUDSON HOPED TO FIND A ROUTE NORTH OF RUSSIA.

Hudson's Second Voyage

Greenland

Svalbard (Norway)

Novaya Zemiya

Sweden

Finland

Iceland

Norway

England

Ireland

Denmark

■ Second Voyage in 1608 A.D.
■ First Voyage in 1607 A.D.

ONCE AGAIN, ICE ALMOST CRUSHED THE SHIP. HUDSON WAS ABLE TO GUIDE THE SHIP TO CALMER WATERS. ICE WAS A CONTINUING DANGER, THOUGH, AND ISLANDS BLOCKED THE WAY.

IF HE FINDS A PASSAGE, WE COULD ALL BE RICH.

WE WOULD BE CRUSHED BY ICE FIRST!

LET'S GET BACK TO THE SHIP.

HUDSON TURNED WEST TOWARD NORTH AMERICA. HIS MEN SAW HE WAS NOT GOING HOME AND THREATENED TO MUTINY. BY AUGUST 1608, HUDSON HAD NO CHOICE. HE WAS FORCED TO RETURN TO ENGLAND.

IT WILL LEAD ONLY TO MORE ICE!

WE WANT TO GO HOME BEFORE WE ARE ALL KILLED!

WE ARE IN OPEN SEAS AGAIN. LET US SEARCH FOR ANOTHER ROUTE.

NO ONE WANTED TO GIVE HUDSON MONEY FOR ANOTHER EXPEDITION. HOWEVER, GEOGRAPHERS LIKE SAMUEL PURCHASE WERE EXCITED ABOUT THE INFORMATION HUDSON BROUGHT BACK.

YOU BROUGHT BACK IMPORTANT GEOGRAPHICAL INFORMATION! CHEER UP. YOU SHOULD NOT BE SO SAD.

I AM A FAILURE. NO ONE BELIEVES I CAN FIND THE ROUTE.

FINALLY, DUTCH MERCHANTS IN THE DUTCH EAST INDIA COMPANY AGREED TO SPONSOR HUDSON. IF HE WAS RIGHT ABOUT A SHORTCUT TO ASIA, THE NETHERLANDS COULD BECOME VERY RICH AND POWERFUL.

IS IT WORTH THE RISK? HE HAS FAILED TWICE BEFORE.

WE NEED TO FIND A BETTER ROUTE BEFORE ENGLAND OR FRANCE DOES.

IF ANYONE CAN FIND ONE, IT WILL BE HUDSON.

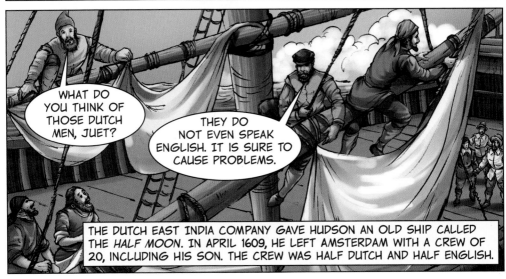

WHAT DO YOU THINK OF THOSE DUTCH MEN, JUET?

THEY DO NOT EVEN SPEAK ENGLISH. IT IS SURE TO CAUSE PROBLEMS.

THE DUTCH EAST INDIA COMPANY GAVE HUDSON AN OLD SHIP CALLED THE HALF MOON. IN APRIL 1609, HE LEFT AMSTERDAM WITH A CREW OF 20, INCLUDING HIS SON. THE CREW WAS HALF DUTCH AND HALF ENGLISH.

HUDSON STARTED SAILING TOWARD RUSSIA, AS THE DUTCH EAST INDIA COMPANY WANTED. SOON HE DECIDED TO SAIL WEST TOWARD NORTH AMERICA INSTEAD.

I WANT TO EXPLORE THE COAST. I BELIEVE THERE IS A PASSAGE FARTHER SOUTH.

HE WAS PROBABLY PLANNING THIS ALL ALONG. WHY ELSE WOULD HE HAVE THESE MAPS?

HUDSON CONVINCED THE CREW THAT IT WOULD BE AN EASIER TRIP.

NORTH AMERICA IS NOT VERY WIDE. ONCE WE FIND THE PASSAGE, IT SHOULD NOT TAKE LONG TO REACH ASIA. THE WEATHER WILL BE WARMER THERE, TOO.

BY JULY, THE *HALF MOON* HAD REACHED NEWFOUNDLAND, CANADA. THE MEN CAUGHT A LOT OF FISH. THEY WERE ABLE TO ADD FRESH FOOD AND WATER TO THEIR SUPPLIES.

IT SURE IS NICE TO HAVE FRESH FOOD.

MAYBE THE CAPTAIN WAS RIGHT ABOUT HAVING AN EASY TRIP FROM NOW ON.

WELL, HE WAS WRONG ABOUT THE WEATHER! I HAVE NEVER SEEN SUCH THICK FOG.

Hudson's Voyage Down the Coast of North America

Island of Newfoundland

New York Harbor

North Carolina

Atlantic Ocean

■ Hudson's Route

HUDSON CONTINUED DOWN THE COAST OF NORTH AMERICA. HE WAS LOOKING FOR A WATERWAY LARGE ENOUGH TO BE THE NORTHWEST PASSAGE. HE FIRST SAILED SOUTH, BUT THEN HE TURNED NORTH AGAIN.

ON SEPTEMBER 2, THE SHIP REACHED WHAT WE KNOW TODAY AS NEW YORK HARBOR. THERE, HUDSON FOUND THE ENTRANCE TO A WIDE RIVER. HE THOUGHT IT MIGHT BE THE PASSAGE.

AS HUDSON SAILED UP THE RIVER, THE BEAUTY OF THE RIVER VALLEY AMAZED HIM, IT WAS RICH, **FERTILE** LAND FILLED WITH WILDLIFE. HE CLAIMED IT AS A DUTCH TERRITORY.

I HOPE THIS IS THE PASSAGE TO ASIA, FATHER. THIS IS A **BOUNTIFUL** LAND.

YES. THE DUTCH WOULD BE VERY PLEASED TO HAVE A ROUTE AND LAND LIKE THIS.

DURING HUDSON'S VOYAGE, HE MET DIFFERENT NATIVE AMERICAN TRIBES. MANY WERE FRIENDLY AND TRADED FOOD AND FURS FOR **TRINKETS**. THEY HAD MET EUROPEANS BEFORE. MANY FRENCH TRADERS HAD PASSED THROUGH.

THESE FURS WILL SELL FOR A PRETTY PENNY BACK IN ENGLAND, EH, JUET?

THEY ARE WORTH MORE THAN THE MIRRORS AND BLANKETS WE ARE TRADING.

ONE MAHICAN CHIEF INVITED HUDSON TO A MEAL. THEY ATE CORN, PIGEONS, DOGS, AND BERRIES. THE ENGLISH HAD NEVER SEEN CORN BEFORE. THEY CALLED IT INDIAN WHEAT.

THE PEOPLE HERE SEEM VERY FRIENDLY AND GIVING.

THEY DO NOW, BUT I DO NOT TRUST THEM.

IN OCTOBER, THE *HALF MOON* REACHED THE MOUTH OF THE RIVER. HUDSON THOUGHT ABOUT SPENDING THE WINTER IN NEWFOUNDLAND.

IF WE WAIT OUT THE WINTER, THE WEATHER WILL SOON GET WARMER. THEN WE CAN EXPLORE MORE WITHOUT HAVING TO START A NEW VOYAGE.

I HOPE THE CAPTAIN WILL NOT FORCE US TO KEEP GOING.

THIS VOYAGE HAS BEEN TOO LONG ALREADY.

THE CREW, THOUGH, HAD BEEN AWAY FROM HOME A LONG TIME. THEY HAD ALREADY FACED MANY DANGERS. HUDSON WORRIED THAT HIS MEN MIGHT MUTINY IF HE STAYED.

HE RETURNED TO ENGLAND IN NOVEMBER 1609. NO ONE IS SURE WHY HE DID NOT GO STRAIGHT TO THE NETHERLANDS.

IT'S GOOD TO BE BACK WHERE I CAN UNDERSTAND EVERYONE.

AYE. . . . AND WHERE THE BREAD AND CHEESE ARE NOT MOLDY!

HE WROTE TO THE DUTCH EAST INDIA COMPANY TO TELL THEM THAT HE HAD FAILED IN HIS MISSION BUT THAT HE HAD DISCOVERED NEW TERRITORY. HE WANTED TO LOOK FOR THE NORTHWEST PASSAGE AGAIN IN THE SPRING.

THEY WILL NOT FUND ANOTHER VOYAGE UNTIL I RETURN THE *HALF MOON* TO THEM.

THEY SHOULD BE PLEASED ABOUT THE LANDS YOU HAVE MAPPED AND CLAIMED FOR THEIR COUNTRY.

BY JULY, THE SHIP WAS BLOCKED BY ICE IN EVERY DIRECTION. STILL, HUDSON MANAGED TO KEEP TRAVELING WEST. HE EXPLORED ISLANDS AND MADE MAPS OF HIS DISCOVERIES.

THE ICE KEEPS US FROM GETTING CLOSE ENOUGH TO LAND.

I DID NOT THINK THERE WOULD STILL BE SO MUCH ICE IN SUMMER.

HUDSON WAS WORRIED, BUT HE SHOWED THE CREW HIS CHARTS. HE TOLD THEM THEY HAD SAILED FARTHER WEST THAN ANY OTHER ENGLISHMEN EVER HAD. ABOUT HALF THE CREW WANTED TO TURN AROUND.

I BELIEVE WE ARE CLOSE TO THE END OF THIS ICY TORMENT. WE HAVE COME SO FAR. WE SHOULD PUSH ON.

I AM CLOSE TO THE END OF MY ROPE! THE CAPTAIN IS OBSESSED.

WE ARE SURE TO DIE IN THIS ICE IF WE GO ON.

AFTER ANOTHER DIFFICULT MONTH, THE *DISCOVERY* REACHED A HUGE BODY OF WATER. AT FIRST, HUDSON THOUGHT THIS WAS THE SEA HE HAD BEEN SEARCHING FOR.

SIR, MANY MEN ARE SICK WITH **SCURVY**. WE MUST LET THEM REST AND LOOK FOR FRESH FOOD.

WE CANNOT REST HERE. WE MUST MOVE ON.

THE CREW BECAME MORE AND MORE UNHAPPY AND FOUGHT AMONG THEMSELVES. ROBERT JUET ARGUED WITH HUDSON AND MADE THREATS. HE WAS PUT ON TRIAL FOR ATTEMPTED MUTINY.

MR. JUET WILL BE REDUCED TO THE RANK OF COMMON SEAMAN. IF HIS SUPPORTERS BEHAVE, THEY WILL NOT BE PUNISHED.

HUDSON CONTINUED EXPLORING THE BAY. BY OCTOBER, IT WAS BITTER COLD AND TOO DARK TO CONTINUE. THE CREW GROUNDED THE DISCOVERY.

HERE IS SOME MOSS WE CAN EAT. HOPEFULLY, WE WON'T STARVE.

IF ONLY THERE WERE SUNLIGHT, I MIGHT HAVE MORE HOPE.

I AM NOT SURE THE CAPTAIN KNOWS WHICH WAY TO GO ANYMORE.

WE HAVE BEEN GONE OVER A YEAR! IT WILL NOT GET BETTER.

THE WATER FINALLY WARMED ENOUGH TO LEAVE IN MAY. SOON, THOUGH, THE SHIP GOT CAUGHT IN ICE AGAIN. AFTER THE CREW FREED IT, THEY WERE SURE THEY WOULD BE GOING HOME. HUDSON INSISTED ON GOING WEST.

HUDSON DIVIDED UP THE LAST SUPPLIES OF FOOD AND WATER. THERE WERE NOT AS MANY CHEESES AS THE SHIP'S **LOG** LISTED. HE THEN HAD THE CREW'S GEAR SEARCHED TO SEE IF ANYONE WAS HIDING FOOD.

I THINK HE IS HIDING THOSE CHEESES IN HIS OWN CABIN!

HE HAS NO RIGHT TO SEARCH OUR PROPERTY!

ON JUNE 22, 1611, GREENE AND JUET LED A MUTINY. THEY PUT HUDSON, HIS SON, AND SEVERAL CREW MEMBERS ON A SMALL BOAT.

THE *DISCOVERY* QUICKLY SAILED AWAY. SIX MEN MADE IT BACK TO ENGLAND. HUDSON AND HIS GROUP WERE NEVER SEEN AGAIN.

HUDSON NEVER FOUND THE NORTHWEST PASSAGE. HOWEVER, HIS COURAGE AND DETERMINATION PROVIDED IMPORTANT DISCOVERIES FOR HIS TIME. HIS NAME LIVES ON IN THE PLACES HE EXPLORED, INCLUDING THE HUDSON RIVER, HUDSON STRAIT, AND HUDSON BAY.

Timeline and Map

1565	Henry Hudson is born around this year.
1585	John Davis leaves on his first voyage in search of a Northwest Passage.
1607	Hudson begins his first voyage, to Greenland and the Svalbard Islands.
1608	Hudson's second voyage, exploring the seas north of Russia, begins.
1609	Hudson departs on his third voyage, during which he travels up the Hudson River in what is now New York.
1610	Hudson's fourth journey, in which he travels north of Canada to Hudson Strait and Hudson Bay, begins.
1611	The crew of the *Discovery* stages a mutiny. Hudson is left adrift on a small boat.
June 1611	Hudson is assumed to have died.

Map of Hudson's Routes

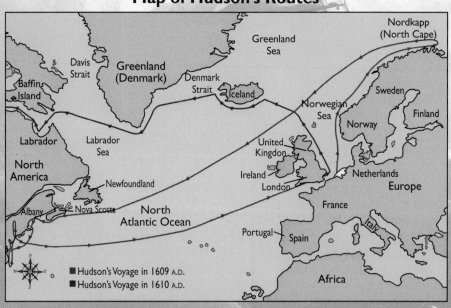

Glossary

astrolabe (AS-truh-layb) An instrument that measures the positions of stars, used to find one's way on the oceans.

bay (BAY) A part of the ocean, close to land, where a ship can stay.

bountiful (BOWN-tih-ful) Plentiful, abundant.

cloves (KLOHVZ) A kind of valuable spice that grows in tropical climates.

fertile (FER-tul) Good for making and growing things.

floes (FLOHZ) Large sheets or masses of floating ice.

investors (in-VES-turz) People who give money for something they hope will bring them more money later.

log (LOG) A record of day-to-day activities.

merchant (MER-chunt) Someone who owns a business that sells goods.

mutiny (MYOO-tuh-nee) A revolt of a ship's crew or of soldiers against their commanding officer.

navigator (NA-vuh-gay-ter) A person who uses maps, the stars, or special tools to travel in a ship, an aircraft, or a rocket.

Northwest Passage (NORTH-west PA-sij) A passage through which one could sail between the North Atlantic Ocean and the Pacific Ocean.

obsessed (ub-SESD) Focused on a thought that completely occupies the mind.

precious (PREH-shus) Having a high value or price.

scurvy (SKUR-vee) A disease in which the teeth fall out from a lack of fruits and vegetables.

sponsor (SPON-ser) A person or company that pays the expenses for someone else, such as an explorer.

territories (TER-uh-tor-eez) Lands that are controlled by a person or a group of people.

trade (TRAYD) The business of buying and selling.

traitor (TRAY-tur) A person who turns against his or her country.

trinkets (TRINK-its) Small, cheap objects.

Index

Websites

Due to the changing nature of Internet links, PowerKids Press has developed an online list of websites related to the subject of this book. This site is updated regularly. Please use this link to access the list:

www.powerkidslinks.com/jgff/huds/